A Time To Talk

Sonja Simpson

BookLeaf
Publishing

Presentation by *BookLeaf Publishing*

Web: www.bookleafpub.com

E-mail: info@bookleafpub.com

ISBN: 9789357212526

First edition 2023

ACKNOWLEDGEMENT

Thank you to my husband Mark for supporting me, also my best friend and author Holly and also to Nicola.

A Time To Talk

There comes a time in your life when things
become too much.
The burden is too much to carry on your own.
Sometimes you need support to help you
through.
Contact us and we will be there for you.

If it be long term or short term support that is
needed, you can come to us.
We will not judge you, we will just listen to your
concerns in a safe environment.
We can support you in whatever way you need
us to.
Just contact us for more details.

We can support you through many seasons in
life.
From autism, unexplained fertility, depression
and anxiety to name a few.
We will support you through as best we can.
We use people who have, or are experiencing the
issues, where possible.

Best Friends

Beautiful
Encouraging
Supportive
Trustworthy

Funny
Reliable
Inspiring
Empathetic
Non-judgemental
Dependable
Sisterly

Christmas

Christmas is a special time of year
A time where we celebrate the birth of Jesus
We spend the four weeks before, in Church
Preparing for the coming of the King.

Christmas time is full of decorations, buying
gifts and sending cards.
Whilst I enjoy the decorating of the tree, and
singing carols.
The choosing of gifts, for those near and dear to
me.
I remember the real meaning of Christmas.

The star on top of the tree, reminds me of the
wise men that followed the star to Bethlehem.
The Inn, a cattle shed – it's only room where
Jesus was born and was laid in a manger.
The Donkey that carried Mary to Bethlehem,
where Jesus our saviour, was born.
The Babe whom was born to save us all, and to
be our best friend, was born in a stable.

Cousins

Cousins are the first children that you make a bond with.
The first friendships that are formed during childhood.
Cousins are always close at hand like a sibling.
My cousins mean the world to me, as an only child.

One cousin is more like a brother that I never had.
We have our own language, including spoonerisms.
We understand each other, even though others don't understand us.
Sometimes, we even get mistaken as a married couple.

Some of my cousins live away from me and even though we are not geographically close,
We are close in our relationships, when we do see each other, we pick up where we left off.
We are bound by our blood relationships, however, due to us being family we also have common ground.

Through thick and thin we are friends and family.

Faith, Hope and Love

Faith is what guides our lives.
Our thoughts and our decisions
Faith is the centre of my core.
Where my deepest desires are stored.

Hope, when life is uncertain.
Hope when life is perfect.
Hope when one door closes.
That God will lead me through another.

Love is the greatest thing that you can receive.
To love with all your heart as Jesus commands.
To love your neighbour, as yourself.
Now these three remain; Faith, Hope and Love.

Fathers and Daughters

The relationship between a Father and Daughter
is special.
Her Daddy is the first man that she learns from.
He also shows her how a man should treat her.
Her first love, her Daddy and role model.

I was very lucky as a child, to have a good
upbringing.
Many children sadly don't have the chance at
that relationship.
Sometimes those who have a bad experience of
parenting,
Continue this throughout the generations.

There are also those who have a bad relationship
with their Dads.
Who decide to make the future different for the
next generation.
Whatever your upbringing, good or bad.
Remember, the future is in your hands.

Friendship

Fun
Reliable
Indispensable
Encouraging
Noble
Dependable
Supportive
Happy
Intelligent
Practical

Godchild

Greatest Godchildren
Often spoilt
Dependent on me
Cherished by me
Held in my heart
Independence looms
Loved as my own
Delighted in their company

Infertility

Involuntary
Never ending
Frustration
Exhausting
Resentment
Tiresome
Incomplete
Lonely
Infuriating
Teardrops
Yearning

It's So Unfair!

Sometimes life is so unfair… I remember saying this as a kid to my parents.
But you know what? It's true and life can be unfair.
At any stage in life others seem to get what they want.
But yet again, it has not happened for me. When will it?

All I ever wanted since I was younger, was to be a Mum.
In science lessons in school, they would talk about safe sex.
One night stands, but yet it looked and sounded so easy.
As I found out later, it is not easy at all.

Marriage

Marriage is an eight letter word that spans a
lifetime.
It's not something that is easy or that you can
give up on.
It's a relationship that takes two people to a lot
of hard work to keep together.
With a little bit of love, patience and
compromise in the mix.

Marriage is for the good and bad times.
The happy and sad times too.
Not forgetting in sickness and in health.
Marriage is not for the feint hearted.

Marriage takes a lot of give and take, and
compromising.
Sacrificing our wants and desires to work
together.
Marriage is the hardest, most difficult
relationship.
But by far, it's the most rewarding.

Migraine VS. Victim

I creep up on my victims when they least expect
me.
Gripping around their head, like a vice.
Squeezing and pulsating sensations go through
their veins.
My victims' bodies lose normal functions, as
they hold their heads.

A wave of nausea flowed through their body, as
their eyes became sore and blurry.
A sensitivity to light and sound, took over their
senses.
They felt an overwhelming feeling of fatigue
and tiredness.
So, she went to her room and got into bed before
falling asleep.

Several hours later, she woke up from her
slumber.
Still feeling the post-migraine fuzziness, as she
slowly wakes.
She takes more painkillers and lays down again
with the gel pillow.
And slowly falls back into a deep sleep.

Later that evening, my victim wakes up feeling better.
No more sensitivity to light and sound.
No more feeling that a vice is around her head.
I failed to stop my victim for more than four hours… maybe next time.

My Mum

My Mum is unique, there is no one like her.
All my friends genuinely love her.
My friends can see my Mum in me.
If I can be half the woman she is, I'll take that.

My Mum is so gentle and loving, generous and
kind.
I realise how lucky I am, to have a Mum with
these qualities.
I had an amazing upbringing, full of love.
Now my heart and life is full of love, and fun to
share with others.

I struggled when I first left home, managing on
my own.
With managing all the bills alone, who knew
how hard it would be?
I did it alone for almost ten years, until I met my
husband.
Now that there are two of us, things have
become so much easier.

Even though I am now married, I still keep in
contact with my Mum.
I hope she is as proud of me as I am of her.

All that remains for me to say is;
Thank you for everything Mum, I love you.

Rest In Peace, Mary

It's almost four years since you went to Heaven.
But it feels like only yesterday.
The whole family were there to say their
goodbyes.
But none of us wanted you to leave.

The day you died, a part of me went with you.
Although I wasn't your biological Daughter, you
treated me like one.
There has been so much I have wanted to tell
you.
But then, I remember you are not here anymore.

Mary was such a loving and gracious lady.
Everyone she met, loved her and she was so
easy to love.
She listened without judgement, every time we
spoke.
Before gently giving her words of advice.

All that remains for me to say is "Mary, we miss
you".
But we find comfort knowing you are with Dad,
'Gordon'.
Your soul mate whom you missed for so long.
Rest in peace Mary, we love you - 14/02/19.

The Day I Met The Kittens

One chilly January day, we headed to pick them
up.
We went into the flat, and there they were.
Two little balls of fluff, with long, white
whiskers.
Also sharp claws, and cute button noses.

We cooed over how cute they were, whilst
'Bobby'.
Whom was called Poppy, sat on my Hubby's
shoulder.
We placed the cat carrier on the floor and waited
for them to get in.
Then we made our way home on the bus, with
both cats in the basket.

On the bus home, all you could hear was a
pitiful meow,
It was coming from the smallest, tortie cat, Lily.
When we got home, I opened the door of the
box,
And waited for them to investigate their new
home.

The two little furballs, came out of the box,
investigated their new surroundings.
Up the lining of the curtains they went, the little
tinkers.
Poppy turned out to be a boy, so Bobby he
became.
Two little fur babies settled down on my chest
and in my heart.

The Long Road

From a very young age, I have wanted children.
I had dreams of getting married in my early
twenties.
Children in my mid to late twenties and beyond.
But little did I imagine how hard it would be to
conceive them.

When we got married ten years ago, we decided
to try.
With us being 30 and 39, we weren't sure if it
would happen.
So the trying began, and after a couple of years
we approached the GP.
We underwent fertility testing, and test after test
came back fine.

At different times in life, we would try again –
desperately hoping I would fall pregnant.
Friends would have a baby, then another, then
another…
I felt useless and so frustrated with it not
working properly.
I would cry tears, after tears of frustration, hurt
and feeling forgotten about.

Ten years later, we are still not parents of a child together.
However, I have two stepsons, eight godchildren and two little fur babies.
I also have special relationships with my friend's children, who I spoil.
I also have my husband's niece and nephews.

Trying To Concieve

My desire for a baby has been since I was
young.
But for some reason, our trying has been long.
Month after Month, disappointment repeats
itself.
As month after month, mother nature intervenes.

Moments of despair flood my heart.
As my body refuses to impart.
There are times when I want my feelings to
depart.
But they are part of who I am, in part.

After years of prayers for my own little one to
love.
I am beginning to think that it will not be.
My body is failing me, by not following the
cycle.
Now I am awaiting further testing.

As time passes, I get more frustrated.
Wondering if a child will be our blessing.
But for now, I am waiting and waiting.
To see if a child will be.

Waiting

Wondering what the future will hold
Aimlessly trying not to fret
Into the future, I gaze
Trying to picture me with a baby
In my arms,
Now, I need to wait and hope in
God.

9 789357 212526